Written by Stephanie Milton, with help from Paul Soares Jr. and Jordan Maron
Designed by Andrea Philpots and Joe Bolder
Illustrations by Joe Bolder, James Burlinson, Steffan Glynn,
Paul Soares Jr., and Jordan Maron
Production by Louis Harvey and Caroline Hancock
Special thanks to Lydia Winters, Owen Hill, and Junkboy
With thanks to the Minecraft testing crew: Laurids Binderup and Sam Foxall

◪MOJANG

Published by arrangement with Mojang and Egmont®

ISBN 978-0-545-82326-5

10 9 8 7 6 5 4 3 2 1   15 16 17 18 19/0

Printed in China   62
First published 2014
This edition first printing 2015

MINECRAFT

© MOJANG

ESSENTIAL HANDBOOK

CONTENTS

InTRODUCTIon

Welcome to the official Minecraft Essential Handbook! It contains all the info you need to stay alive during your first few days. It's packed with tips from creator Notch and developer Jeb as well as well-known Minecraft experts, including Paul Soares Jr., host of the Survive and Thrive YouTube tutorial series, and CaptainSparklez, famous Minecraft YouTuber and creator of the Minecraft Style music video. With the help of this handbook, you'll soon be well on your way toward becoming an expert yourself!

Minecraft is a block-building sandbox game with no set rules, where you can build anything you can possibly imagine. You will begin in the first dimension, the Overworld, where you might find yourself in one of several different environments (or biomes): swamp, extreme hills, taiga, desert, forest, plains, jungle, ice plains, ocean, or even the rare mushroom biome.

From the Overworld you can enter the Nether — a hellish landscape of doom, and the End — a terrifying spit of land in the middle of space, inhabited by the Ender Dragon! There are achievements to earn as you progress through the game. You can play alone or with others. You can play in safe Creative mode, exploring the land and building amazing things, or in Survival or Hardcore mode, hunting and mining, and fighting the monsters that come out at night.

What kind of adventure will you choose? It's up to you!

FILE: NOTCH

FULL NAME: Markus Alexej Persson
ROLE: Minecraft creator, co-founder of Mojang

Notch was born in Stockholm, Sweden, in 1979. He began programming (writing code for games) at the age of seven, and produced his first game at eight! After creating Minecraft he co-founded Mojang to develop the game. Notch has over 1,940,000 Twitter followers. He handed over Minecraft development to Jens Bergensten before Mojang was acquired by Microsoft.

FILE: JEB

FULL NAME: Jens Bergensten
ROLE: Minecraft lead developer

Jeb was born in Sweden in 1979, and took over from Notch as lead developer for Minecraft in 2012. He currently has over 1,220,000 Twitter followers and is well-known for his work on redstone repeaters, wolves, climbing spiders, and pistons.

TIP: STAYING SAFE ONLINE
Playing Minecraft on multiplayer servers is a lot of fun! Here are a few simple rules to help you stay safe, and keep the world of Minecraft a great place to spend time:

- Never give out your real name — don't use it as your username.
- Never give out any of your personal details.
- Never tell anybody which school you go to or how old you are.
- Never tell anybody your password except a parent or guardian.

A SHORT HISTORY OF MInECKArT

2009

MAY: Notch begins working on his game idea, and quits his job to concentrate on it full-time. As work progresses, he calls it Cave Game. He releases the first version to the public and calls it Minecraft. The first accounts are registered and the official MInecraft forum opens.

DECEMBER: Minecraft moves to "in development" stage. Lots of things are added, including crafting.

2010

JANUARY: 100,000 registered Minecrafters!

JUNE: Minecraft reaches Alpha stage. At this point Survival was the only mode available, but game updates began to come thick and fast. Sales of the game hit 200,000.

AUGUST: First ever MineCon is held in Washington state. 50 people attend.

DECEMBER: Minecraft wins Indie Game of the Year from IndieDB. Minecraft Beta is released. Additions include egg-throwing and constant splash text on the main menu page.

2011

MARCH: Minecraft wins GDC Award for Best Debut Game, Best Downloadable Game, and Game Innovation Spotlight.

JULY: 10 million registered Minecrafters!

OCTOBER: The Pocket Edition of Minecraft is released for Android.

NOVEMBER: MineCon held in Las Vegas. 5,000 people attend. During MineCon, Minecraft 1.0.0 is released and Minecraft is officially out of Beta. New additions include the Ender Dragon, mooshrooms, and villagers.

A SHORT HISTORY OF MInecraft ... CONTINUED

2012

MARCH: Minecraft version 1.2.1 is released. New additions include the jungle biome, ocelots, cats, and iron golems.

MAY: Minecraft for Xbox 360 is released. It sells 400,000 copies in the first 24 hours.

NOVEMBER: MineCon is held at Disneyland Paris. There are 6,500 attendees.

DECEMBER: Minecraft sells 453,000 copies of the game across all platforms on Christmas Eve alone!

2013

JANUARY: Minecraft sales reach 20 million on PC/Mac, Xbox 360, and mobile devices.

MARCH: Minecraft version 1.5 (aka "The Redstone Update") is released. New additions include redstone-related blocks such as activator rails, redstone blocks, daylight sensors, comparators, trapped chests, and weighted pressure plates, as well as Nether quartz and quartz blocks.

APRIL: Minecraft Pocket Edition and PC/Mac Editions have sold more than 10 million copies each.

JULY: Minecraft version 1.6 (aka "The Horse Update") is released. New additions include horses, donkeys, mules, skeleton and zombie horses, horse armor, hay bales, carpet, and hardened and stained clay blocks.

OCTOBER: Minecraft version 1.7.2 (aka "The Update that Changed the World") is released. It includes new biomes, blocks, and types of fish.

DECEMBER: Minecraft for PlayStation 3 is released.

2014

JUNE: Sales of Console Editions surpass sales for PC/Mac Edition. Across all platforms, 54 million copies of the game have been sold.

AUGUST: Minecraft version 1.8 (aka "The Bountiful Update") is released. New additions include diorite, andesite, granite, banner, slime, and barrier blocks; ocean monuments in deep ocean biomes; rabbits, and changes to the enchanting system.

SEPTEMBER: Mojang is acquired by Microsoft. Minecraft: Xbox One and Minecraft: PlayStation 4 Editions are released.

PLATFORMS

Minecraft is available on a number of platforms. You can play on your computer (either PC or Mac), on Xbox and PlayStation consoles, or on pocket devices. The game varies depending on which platform you use.

SINGLE PLAYER AND MULTIPLAYER

You can play alone in single player, or ask a friend to show you what to do in multiplayer. For the purposes of this book, we have assumed you'll be starting out on your own in single player.

CREATIVE, SURVIVAL, AND HARDCORE MODES

You'll be asked to choose one of the following modes.

In **Creative mode**, no monsters will attack you, you'll be able to fly around, and you'll have a full inventory of items. This is great if you want unlimited resources to build amazing creations and buildings without having them blown up by creepers every five minutes.

In **Survival mode** you get to have loads of fun fighting off monsters. You can choose to play in easy, normal, hard, or peaceful difficulty. If you're a beginner, it's best to start off with normal difficulty.

In **Hardcore mode** the difficulty is locked on hard, and you only get one life. The decision is yours!

LEVELS

As you play you will earn experience points, which will enable you to level up. The green bar shows your current level, so you can see how close you are to reaching the next level. Experience points are earned when you mine items and kill monsters. Experience orbs will appear and you can pick them up.

 DID YOU KNOW? There are 17 experience points to each of the first 16 levels of the game. Once you reach level 17, the number of points needed to rank up increases with each level you achieve, making progress more difficult.

 TIP: Experience points will come in useful when you learn how to enchant items to improve their performance. You can use your experience points as a method of payment to enchant objects like tools, weapons, and armor.

CONTROLS

Controls

Button 1	Attack	Button 2	Use Item
W	Forward	A	Left
S	Back	D	Right
SPACE	Jump	LSHIFT	Sneak
Q	Drop	E	Inventory
T	Chat	TAB	List Players
Button 3	Pick Block	SLASH	Command

RIGHT CLICK / BUTTON 2

LEFT CLICK / BUTTON 1

SCROLL / BUTTON 3

DID YOU KNOW? There's a 3-D mode! Go to Options, Video Settings, then turn 3-D Anaglyph mode on. All you need are some red-and-blue 3-D glasses.

TIP: Hold your Shift key down when exploring ledges and cliff tops. This will allow you to sneak around and will stop you falling over the edge.

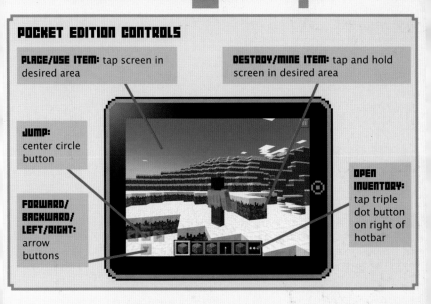

POCKET EDITION CONTROLS

PLACE/USE ITEM: tap screen in desired area

DESTROY/MINE ITEM: tap and hold screen in desired area

JUMP: center circle button

FORWARD/ BACKWARD/ LEFT/RIGHT: arrow buttons

OPEN INVENTORY: tap triple dot button on right of hotbar

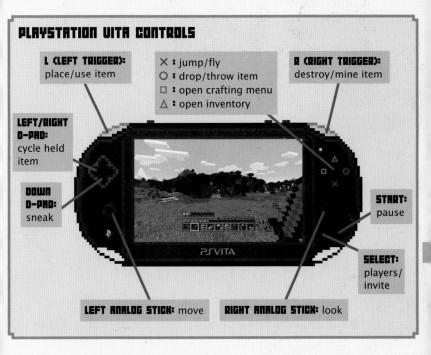

PLAYSTATION VITA CONTROLS

L (LEFT TRIGGER): place/use item

✕ : jump/fly
◯ : drop/throw item
▢ : open crafting menu
△ : open inventory

R (RIGHT TRIGGER): destroy/mine item

LEFT/RIGHT D-PAD: cycle held item

DOWN D-PAD: sneak

START: pause

SELECT: players/ invite

LEFT ANALOG STICK: move

RIGHT ANALOG STICK: look

CONTROLS ... CONTINUED

XBOX ONE CONTROLS

LT (LEFT TRIGGER): place/use item

RT (RIGHT TRIGGER): destroy/mine item

LB/RB (LEFT BUMPER/ RIGHT BUMPER): change the selected item

A: jump/fly
B: drop/throw item
X: open crafting menu
Y: open inventory

LEFT ANALOG STICK (MOVE FORWARD TWICE IN QUICK SUCCESSION): run

LEFT ANALOG STICK (PRESSED DOWN): fly lower in Creative mode or change camera angle

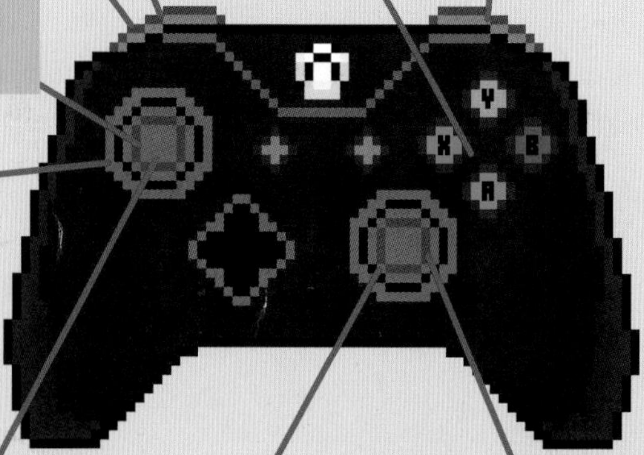

LEFT ANALOG STICK: move

RIGHT ANALOG STICK: look

RIGHT ANALOG STICK (PRESSED DOWN): sneak/walk

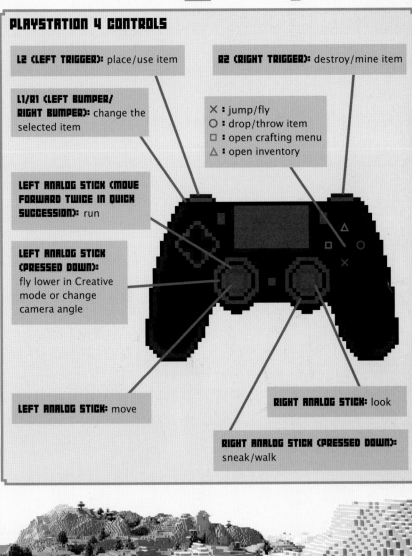

PLAYSTATION 4 CONTROLS

L2 (LEFT TRIGGER): place/use item

R2 (RIGHT TRIGGER): destroy/mine item

L1/R1 (LEFT BUMPER/ RIGHT BUMPER): change the selected item

✕ : jump/fly
◯ : drop/throw item
◻ : open crafting menu
△ : open inventory

LEFT ANALOG STICK (MOVE FORWARD TWICE IN QUICK SUCCESSION): run

LEFT ANALOG STICK (PRESSED DOWN): fly lower in Creative mode or change camera angle

LEFT ANALOG STICK: move

RIGHT ANALOG STICK: look

RIGHT ANALOG STICK (PRESSED DOWN): sneak/walk

INVENTORY

Your inventory is the place where everything you mine and collect is stored. You can open your inventory at any time during the game. See pages 14-17 to check how to do it on your device.

CRAFTING GRID
Place ingredients here to craft them into useful items and tools.

OUTPUT SQUARE
Your newly crafted item will appear here.

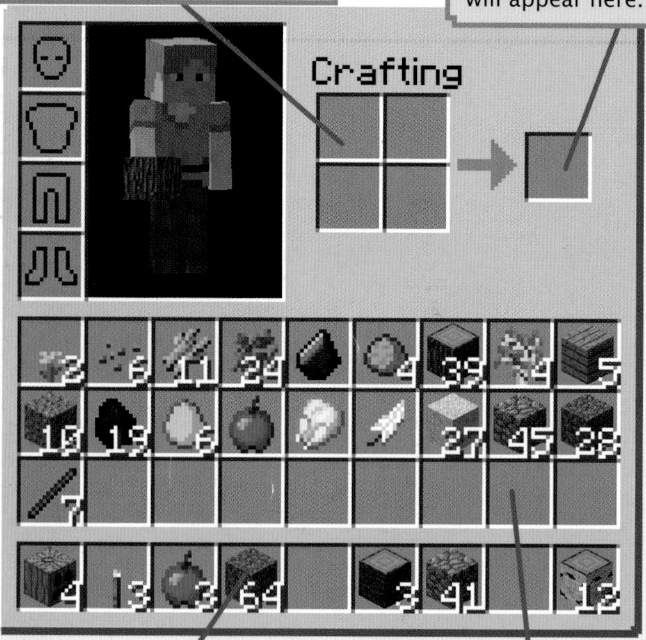

Crafting

ITEMS
Most Items are stackable up to a maximum of 64 per slot.

STORAGE
There are 27 storage slots available in your inventory.

DID YOU KNOW? Crafting is trickier on PC/Mac Edition than on Console or Pocket Editions. The Console and Pocket Editions tell you what you can make with the items you have, but on a PC or Mac you have to figure it out for yourself.

When you exit your inventory, a line of 9 hotkey slots will appear at the bottom of your screen. This is your hotbar, which is a mini-inventory where you can keep the things you use most often.

Just move an item from your inventory into one of the hotkey slots to assign it. When you select a slot, the item saved in that slot will appear in your hand, ready to be used.

 TIP: A well-organized hotbar might just save your life. Keep at least one weapon and one source of food in your hotbar at all times so you can defend yourself against a hostile enemy or quickly fill up your food bar.

SURVIVAL MODE:
FIRST MOMENTS

You will begin your game, or spawn, at daybreak in a randomly generated environment. Take a moment to look around and see what resources you've got to work with.

If you're lucky, you'll find yourself in an area full of natural resources like trees, rocks, water, and animals that you can use to make useful items. If you're unlucky, you might find yourself on a tiny island in the middle of a vast ocean with no resources and nothing useful in sight.

LUCKY SPAWN

Trees — check. Rock — check. Water — check. Animals — check. Perfect!

UNLUCKY SPAWN

Stranded in the middle of the ocean on a tiny island. Uh-oh . . .

DID YOU KNOW? If you die, you reappear at your spawn point. Mark a trail from your spawn point to the shelter you will build. That way, if you die, you can always get back to the safety of your home quickly.

1

Daytime only lasts for 10 minutes. The sun rises in the east and sets in the west — check where it is now and keep track of its progress through the sky so you know how close it is to nightfall, which is when the monsters come out. More about them later! When you've found some more resources, you'll be able to craft a clock. (See page 86 for recipe.)

2

Your main priorities are to find a few basic resources and a good spot to build a shelter for the night to keep you safe from monsters. Head for the nearest tree and hit the trunk repeatedly with your hand. After a few moments the section of the trunk you're hitting will fall away as a small cube of wood, which you can pick up. It will then appear in your inventory.

TIP: When harvesting trees, the wood blocks should automatically zoom toward you and pop into your inventory. If they don't, you might not be standing close enough. Just step forward a few paces to pick them up.

3

Repeat Step 2 until you have at least 15 blocks in your hotbar. Open your inventory and drag 1 block of wood into any of the crafting squares to create 4 planks of wood.

WOOD PLANKS RECIPE

4

Move the planks into your inventory to save them, then drag them back into the crafting area. Four planks will make a crafting table, which is a very useful tool that you'll use constantly.

CRAFTING TABLE RECIPE

PAUL SOARES JR.
MY FIRST DAY IN MINECRAFT
SURVIVAL SINGLE PLAYER (SSP)

I purchased Minecraft in July 2010. Notch had just released version Alpha 1.0.3, which added monster sounds and cave noises to the game for the first time. This was a time before chickens and cows even existed. It was a time when zombies dropped feathers. A time before the hunger bar and auto-healing. A time before comfy beds to sleep through the scary night! Aye, it was a long time ago, in a long-forgotten age . . .

My first day in Minecraft started well. The landscape was beautiful with its bright grasslands, sandy beaches, dense forests, rolling green hills, and tall mountains with waterfalls cascading down their stony cliff faces.

I just started wandering, exploring every nook and cranny. It felt like I was on some sort of fantastic journey in a wild, undiscovered place. A brave new world that no other living soul had ever stepped foot upon (not counting the few pigs and sheep I'd encountered, of course).

Then the sun sank beneath the horizon and nightfall covered the land in darkness. That's when I discovered I was not alone in my world and that I shared it with a variety of terrible monsters. Zombies, skeletons, and giant spiders were literally popping out of the dark all around me! Not surprisingly, they didn't seem particularly interested in sharing their world. Rather, they were far more concerned with making me a snack. Their snack!

The chase was on! The monsters were persistent and pursued me this way and that. I ran for my life but quickly realized there was no place to go. They were everywhere in the dark of night and inside caves as well. I had no light source, no shelter to hide in, and no weapon. So I did the one thing I could do: I continued to run!

It was during this mad dash for survival that I met my first creeper. I had no idea what it was since it didn't resemble any typical monster or creature from familiar lore or legend. At first glance it appeared to be harmless; it didn't have any sort of visible weapons. Heck, it didn't even have any arms and I must admit, it was even a little bit cute.

Maybe it's friendly, I reasoned. I moved toward it, thinking it might help me against the monsters still giving chase. As I got closer to this odd creature it started making a hissing sound.

Hmm, that actually sounds more like a "sizzle," I thought to myself as I came face-to-face with this strange, adorable creature. And then it started to . . . expand.

KABOOM!

The creeper exploded and blew me to smithereens and the screen reported: Game Over!

Thus ended my first day in Minecraft.

I eventually decided to make my own tutorials to help people not get eaten on their first night.

Check out youtube.com/paulsoaresjr

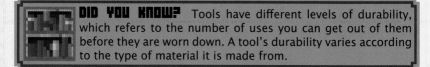

WOODEN TOOLS

Tools are essential for mining as they allow you to destroy blocks faster and more efficiently. Without them, you're not going to get very far at all, so you need to craft a basic set as early as possible.

When you first start playing you only have wood, so the first tool you need to make is a wooden pickaxe. This will enable you to mine stone, which you need to create stone tools to mine more valuable substances.

> **DID YOU KNOW?** Tools have different levels of durability, which refers to the number of uses you can get out of them before they are worn down. A tool's durability varies according to the type of material it is made from.

Place your crafting table on the ground in front of you and interact with it. You now have a 3x3 crafting grid to work with, which means you can craft more complicated items.

STICKS RECIPE

First, make sticks for the handle. Two planks (one on top of the other) will give you 4 sticks.

WOODEN PICKAXE RECIPE

Add 3 planks of wood to form the head of the pickaxe. A wooden pickaxe will mine basic ores and blocks like coal ore and cobblestone, but not valuable ores like redstone, gold, or diamond.

Durability: 60

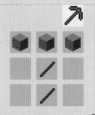

WOODEN AXE RECIPE

An axe will allow you to chop wood more quickly.

Durability: **60**

WOODEN SHOVEL RECIPE

A shovel will dig dirt, sand, gravel, clay, and snow more quickly.

Durability: **60**

TIP: You can repair worn-down tools by combining 2 tools of the same type in your crafting grid. When combined, they'll produce 1 tool with increased durability, plus you'll have another free slot in your inventory.

Now you're all ready to start mining stone!

TORCHES

Sunset is approaching and you need a light source . . . fast. Hostile monsters like spiders, creepers, and zombies will spawn in dark areas, including your shelter. Scary stuff.

Eek! A giant arachnid that can see in the dark!

1

To make torches you'll need wood and coal. Look for a rock face and see if you can spot any coal ore. It looks like stone with black flecks and is commonly found in cliff faces as well as belowground.

2

Use your wooden pickaxe to destroy a block of coal ore until it drops a lump of coal. Repeat until you have several lumps so you can make lots of torches. You can never have too many torches.

3 TORCH RECIPE

Torches can be crafted without a crafting table because they require only 2 ingredients: sticks and coal. A stick and 1 lump of coal will make 4 torches that can be placed on the top or the side of solid blocks. They can't be placed on water, on the side of stairs, or on the bottom of blocks.

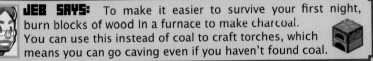

JEB SAYS: To make it easier to survive your first night, burn blocks of wood in a furnace to make charcoal. You can use this instead of coal to craft torches, which means you can go caving even if you haven't found coal.

FURNACE RECIPE

Arrange 8 blocks of cobblestone in your crafting grid to make a furnace.

JACK-O'-LANTERN RECIPE

Torches can be crafted into jack-o'-lanterns by combining them with pumpkins.

TIP: You can use torches to melt snow and ice to create a safe path.

DID YOU KNOW? You might be able to find torches in strongholds, abandoned mineshafts, and NPC (Non-Player Character) villages.

SHELTER

Time to make a shelter to keep you safe from monsters during the night. Don't forget to bring your crafting table with you because you're going to need it once you're inside!

1

Find a suitable spot in a rock face. You could use the area where you've been mining coal as a starting point, then dig farther in. You'll need plenty of space inside for your crafting table and various other items, as well as extra space to move around.

2

Use the rock you mine to build a wall between you and the outside world. Dig an L-shaped space in the rock so you can hide around a corner in case a skeleton decides to shoot at you through the window.

 NOTCH SAYS: Your first-day shelter doesn't have to be pretty; you can work on it the next day. Just make sure you have a place you can hide from all the creepy-crawlies. Leave 1 block open so you can spot monsters and see when daylight returns.

3

Place a torch on each wall inside your shelter. Having a light source will ensure no hostile monsters spawn inside your shelter. Monsters can spawn anywhere that is dark enough.

CHEST RECIPE

Your inventory slots will eventually fill up, so make a chest to store excess items.

DID YOU KNOW?

A single chest can store up to 27 stacks of items/blocks. Placing 2 chests next to each other will give you a double chest with 54 storage slots.

4

Place the chest in your shelter. You can use it to store valuable items that you want to keep safe, or items that you aren't using right now.

STONE TOOLS AND WEAPONS

There's no time to relax during your first night. While you're hiding out in your shelter, you need to craft some more advanced tools for your second day so that you can gather the resources you need.

Access your crafting table again. You're going to craft a range of stone tools and weapons that will make Day 2 much easier than Day 1. Luckily, you're surrounded by stone, so you should have plenty of material.

Stone tools last longer than wooden tools, and allow you to mine substances like stone and ores much more quickly.

STONE PICKAXE RECIPE

A stone pickaxe is ideal for mining stone, coal ore, and iron ore.

Durability: 132

STONE SHOVEL RECIPE

A stone shovel is ideal for digging grass, dirt, sand, and clay.

Durability: 132

STONE AXE RECIPE

A stone axe will make chopping wood much easier.

Durability: 132

STONE SWORD RECIPE

Make a stone sword to defend yourself against hostile monsters.

Durability: 132

Save your tools in your hotbar for easy access, then check out all the experience points you've earned as a result of your crafting spree!

TIP: When mining for stone, never dig straight down. This is the Number One Rule in Minecraft. You could fall into lava, a cave system, or a dungeon, all of which could result in your untimely death. Never dig directly above your head, either.

 DID YOU KNOW? When you've gathered enough resources you'll be able to craft iron, gold, and diamond tools. Each substance has a different durability and destroys blocks at a different rate. Diamond tools are the most effective and most durable.

A stone pickaxe helps you mine coal ore more quickly.

H=nLTH nuu ru....

I n Survival and Hardcore modes you'll need to keep an eye on your health and food bars. They sit just above your hotbar. The health bar is made up of 10 hearts and the food bar of 10 shanks.

Your health bar will go down if you begin to starve or take damage. Your food bar will go down as you use up energy. Be warned: If your health bar goes down to zero, you will die.

DID YOU KNOW? Different types of food will restore different amounts of food points (1 point equals half a shank). A potato will restore 1 food point, but a cake will restore 14 points. See page 37 for a cake recipe.

When Day 2 finally breaks (assuming you're still alive, which you should be if you've been paying attention!) your next priority will be to find food. Fortunately, it's likely to be all around you.

It's impossible to be greedy and overeat in Minecraft, so don't even try. You won't be able to eat food when your food bar is full or if you are playing in Creative mode. You can only eat when you need to fill up your food bar.

HUNTING ANIMALS
BY PAUL SOARES JR.

I usually feel guilty when I need to kill animals for their resources. Sometimes, however, an animal will employ special tactics to confuse and frustrate you to the very point that you can't wait to kill it! I remember a particularly annoying cow in my early days of Survival. I had searched far and wide for leather but could not find any cows. I was nearly ready to give up when I spied a cow on the edge of a cliff.

The cliff face was too sheer to climb, so I used the "gravel elevator" trick (jumping and placing gravel below you) to raise myself to the cow's height. As I reached the top of the cliff, the cow decided to employ his secret evasion tactic: JUMP! The cow landed far below with a crunch. I shouted angry words and dug my way back down to the ground. The cow seemed to be out of escape tricks so I killed it, and it went *poof* and dropped . . . nothing!

And the moral of the story?

When you go hunting, bring a bow.

MEAT

Meat restores lots of food points. Look for a cow, a pig, a chicken, a sheep, or a rabbit and hit it repeatedly until it dies. You'll know it's dead because it will turn red, then fall over and disappear.

It's best to cook meat before eating it to increase the food points it will restore. Plus, if you eat raw chicken there's a chance you'll get food poisoning. Once you've collected some raw meat, head back to your shelter and cook it in your furnace. Just place coal, charcoal, or wood underneath the flame symbol and the raw food on top. After a few moments it will be ready to eat. It's a good idea to keep some cooked food in your hotbar when you go exploring, in case you need to fill up urgently.

RAW		
Beef	3	Food Points
Pork chop	3	Food Points
Chicken	2	Food Points
Mutton	2	Food Points
Rabbit	3	Food Points

COOKED		
Steak	8	Food Points
Pork chop	8	Food Points
Chicken	6	Food Points
Mutton	6	Food Points
Rabbit	5	Food Points

TIP: If the first animal you kill doesn't drop any meat, look for another. The animal will try to run away from you once you hit it, so you'll need to be fast!

FISH

Raw fish are an unlimited and reliable source of food. On a rainy day you can catch a fish every 15 seconds on average. To catch a fish, all you'll need is a fishing rod and a boat.

There are 3 types of edible fish that can be caught with a fishing rod: raw fish, raw salmon, and clownfish. You can eat all 3 types of fish raw, but raw fish and raw salmon can be cooked in a furnace.

FISHING ROD RECIPE

You can craft a fishing rod from sticks and string.

Durability: 65

You can get string from killing spiders, or destroying cobwebs or trip wires.

RAW

Fish	2	Food Points
Salmon	2	Food Points
Clownfish	1	Food Point

COOKED

Fish	5	Food Points
Salmon	6	Food Points

Find an area of water and use your fishing rod to cast your bait into the water. The bobber will dip when you've caught something, then you can reel it in. To increase the number of food points they provide, cook raw fish and raw salmon in your furnace.

FRUIT AND VEGETABLES

F ruit and vegetables are an ideal food source if you can't find any animals or if you just don't want to kill a poor defenseless creature. And they're all around you, if you know where to look.

APPLES

Apples are a great food source since you can find them in trees and don't need to grow or prepare them. Find some oak trees, then destroy the leaves until an apple falls out.

Food Points: 4

MELON SLICES

Melon blocks are found in jungle biomes, and their seeds are in chests in abandoned mineshafts. When they're destroyed, melon blocks drop 3-7 melon slices.

Food Points: 2

CARROTS

Carrots are sometimes dropped by zombies when they die, but can frequently be found in NPC village farms, just sitting there ready for the taking.

Food Points: 3

POTATOES

Like carrots, potatoes are rare drops from zombies and can be found in NPC village farms. A potato can be baked in a furnace, which increases its food points.

Food Points: 1 raw 5 baked

With just a few base ingredients and a bit of know-how, you can expand your Minecraft menu to include a variety of baked goods and sweet treats, with high food point values. Yum!

BREAD RECIPE

A loaf of bread can be crafted from just 3 wheat (farmed from seeds dropped by long grass).

Food Points: 5

PUMPKIN PIE RECIPE

You need 1 pumpkin, sugar (crafted from sugar cane), and 1 egg (dropped by chickens).

Food Points: 8

COOKIE RECIPE

You need wheat and cocoa beans (found in jungle biomes as pods on the side of jungle trees).

Food Points: 2

CAKE RECIPE

You need 3 buckets of milk (obtained by using a bucket on a cow), 2 sugar, wheat (see pages 78–79), and 1 egg.

Food Points: 14

BUCKET RECIPE

You can craft a bucket from 3 iron ingots. Buckets can hold water, lava, or milk.

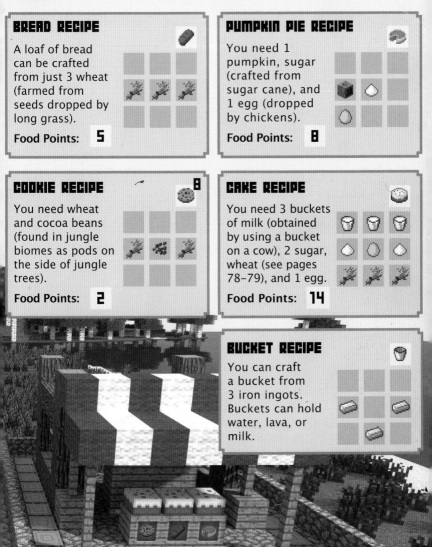

CRAFTING A BED

You've made it through your first night and the second night is approaching fast. Take some time during your second day to find wool to craft a bed, as it will make the nights much easier.

Using your bed at night allows you to sleep right through to the next morning in complete safety. And that means you can avoid a whole night of potential hostile monster attacks. Awesome!

There are several ways to obtain wool:

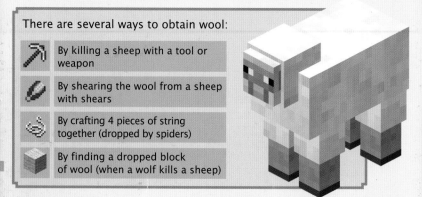

	By killing a sheep with a tool or weapon
	By shearing the wool from a sheep with shears
	By crafting 4 pieces of string together (dropped by spiders)
	By finding a dropped block of wool (when a wolf kills a sheep)

SHEEP SHEARING

If you're feeling kind and decide to shear a sheep rather than kill one, you'll be rewarded for your good deed. They will drop 1-3 blocks of wool if you shear them, but only 1 block if you kill them. Just use your shears on a sheep. The wool will fall away and you will be able to pick it up.

SHEARS RECIPE

You'll need 2 iron ingots, obtained by smelting iron ore in your furnace.

DID YOU KNOW?

In single player, once you've slept in your bed it will automatically become your spawn point, which means you'll always spawn safely at home.

If you're feeling lazy and try to sleep during the day a message will pop up, saying, "You can only sleep at night."

BED RECIPE

A comfy bed can be crafted from 3 blocks of wool and 3 planks.

Zzzzzz . . .

When you're a little more advanced, you might journey to the Nether or the End. But don't be tempted to place a bed in either dimension, or you'll get an explosive surprise . . .

35

TABLE N. BLOCKS

As you explore, you'll discover new blocks in the unlikeliest of places. Many appear at surface level, but with a little mining skill you can find precious substances deep below ground.

This is a table of basic blocks, divided into various categories. The ores on the left are mainly found below ground — some are very rare. Most of the other blocks occur regularly across the Overworld. The column on the right contains blocks found only in the Nether and End dimensions.

Most of these blocks can be mined and picked up, but air, water, fire, lava, cobweb, bedrock and monster spawner can't.

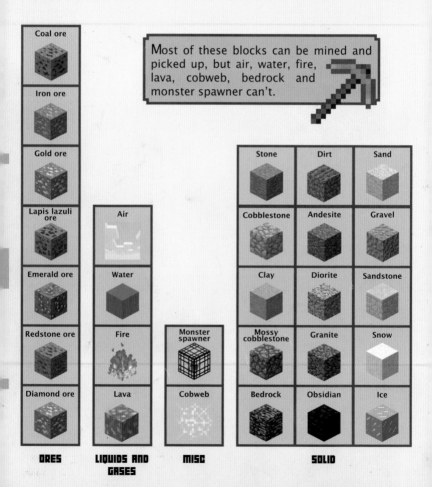

ORES	LIQUIDS AND GASES	MISC	SOLID		
Coal ore					
Iron ore			Stone	Dirt	Sand
Gold ore			Cobblestone	Andesite	Gravel
Lapis lazuli ore	Air		Clay	Diorite	Sandstone
Emerald ore	Water		Mossy cobblestone	Granite	Snow
Redstone ore	Fire	Monster spawner			
Diamond ore	Lava	Cobweb	Bedrock	Obsidian	Ice

Glowstone

Netherrack

Nether wart

Soul sand

Nether brick

Nether quartz

Quartz

End stone

NETHER AND END BLOCKS

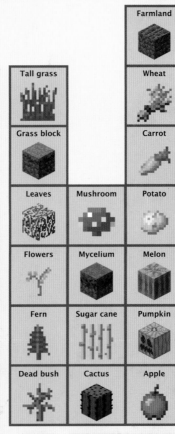

Farmland

Wheat

Carrot

Mushroom | Potato

Mycelium | Melon

Sugar cane | Pumpkin

Cactus | Apple

VEGETATION | **FARM AND FOOD**

Tall grass

Grass block

Leaves

Flowers

Fern

Dead bush

FOLIAGE

Oak

Spruce

Birch

Jungle

Acacia

Dark oak

WOOD BASED

Lily pad

Prismarine

Dark prismarine

Sea lantern

Sponge

WATER BASED

41

A GUIDE TO

MINING BASE ELEMENTS

🅖 BY CAPTAINSPARKLEZ

Gold, redstone, emerald, and diamond are higher-tier ores, and finding them can prove very rewarding. In order to find these materials, you will need to venture underground to a fairly low elevation (level). You'll need an iron pickaxe at the very least to be able to mine these ores. I'd recommend additional weapons and armor in order to successfully fight off the mobs that you'll run into underground.

GOLD ORE

The easiest of the bunch to find, as it generates in fairly large quantities, and can be found at elevations ranging from y=1 all the way to y=31. Once gold ore is mined, it must be smelted in a furnace to make gold ingots, which can be used to make armor and weapons.

REDSTONE ORE

Found between the elevations of y=1 and y=15, and generates in larger quantities than gold between those elevations, making it easier to find. When mined, redstone ore will give you several redstone dust, which can be used later on to create circuits.

TIP: Given the overlapping elevations at which these resources are found, the best place to search for them is between the elevations y=5 and y=10. All 4 ores generate at their maximum rates within that range.

DID YOU KNOW? You can check your coordinates when playing on a PC/Mac by pressing F3 and checking your x (east–west), y (high–low), and z (north–south) coordinates. The y coordinate is useful when mining since it tells you how deep you are. The bottom of the world (the lowest bedrock layer) is y=0 and sea level is y=64.

DIAMOND ORE

Arguably the most useful material in the game, and can be found between the elevations y=1 and y=15 in similar quantities to gold. When mined, diamond ore will give you a diamond, which you need to craft any diamond tool, weapon, or piece of armor.

EMERALD ORE

Only found in extreme hills biomes, between the elevations y=4 and y=31, but in much smaller quantities than any of the others. Mining emerald ore will give you a single emerald, which can be used in villager trades as payment for other items.

MINING: THE GOLDEN RULES

Mining can be a highly dangerous business, but it's also essential if you want to access useful materials. Keep these golden rules in mind and you'll have a much better chance of surviving your subterranean journeys.

1 LOCATION

Try to find an existing cave system rather than digging blindly into the ground. This will save you an incredible amount of time and resources, and hopefully lead you straight to the good stuff.

2 STARTING OUT

Never dig straight up or straight down. You could unearth lava, water, or hostile enemies.

3 SAFETY FIRST

Always carry a bucket of water in your hotbar in case you do fall into lava and catch fire.

4 WATERFALLS

If you're careful, you can swim up and down waterfalls to travel quickly between different levels. Just remember not to stay submerged for too long or you will drown.

7 BUILDING A BASE

If you'll be spending a lot of time in a particular cave system, build yourself a base. It's always useful to have somewhere safe where you can craft and smelt useful items.

6 SUPPLIES

Don't forget to take plenty of wood. Without it, you won't be able to craft tools or torches.

5 HEALTH

Remember to bring food — all that mining will take its toll on your food and health bars, and you'll need to fill up.

MOBS

obs (short for "mobiles") are creatures that have a degree of intelligence and behave independently. This includes monsters and villagers as well as animals. Most mobs drop useful items.

Some mobs are passive and won't attack you even if you attack them. A few are neutral and will only become hostile if you attack them first. But many are hostile and will attack you as soon as they see you, so it's very important that you learn where to find them and what they look like.

ANIMALS

Mostly passive creatures, animals are a handy source of useful materials.

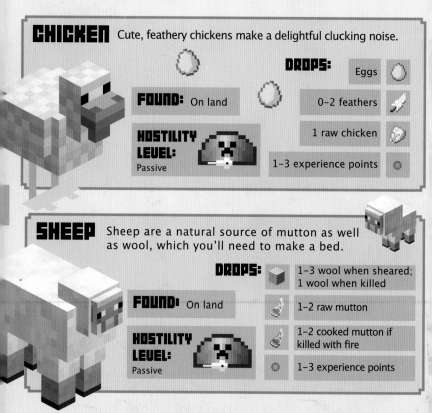

CHICKEN
Cute, feathery chickens make a delightful clucking noise.

FOUND: On land

HOSTILITY LEVEL: Passive

DROPS:
- Eggs
- 0-2 feathers
- 1 raw chicken
- 1-3 experience points

SHEEP
Sheep are a natural source of mutton as well as wool, which you'll need to make a bed.

FOUND: On land

HOSTILITY LEVEL: Passive

DROPS:
- 1-3 wool when sheared; 1 wool when killed
- 1-2 raw mutton
- 1-2 cooked mutton if killed with fire
- 1-3 experience points

COW

Cows may be the noisiest mob in the Overworld, but they're a great source of materials.

DROPS:

0–2 pieces of leather	Milk if you use a bucket while alive
1–3 pieces of raw beef	1–3 experience points
1–3 pieces of steak if killed with fire	

FOUND: On land

HOSTILITY LEVEL: Passive

MOOSHROOM

Red and white cows covered in mushrooms.

FOUND: In the mushroom island biome

DROPS:

	Mushroom soup if you use a bowl while alive
5 mushrooms if sheared	1–3 pieces of steak if killed with fire
0–2 pieces of leather	1–3 experience points
1–3 pieces of raw beef	

HOSTILITY LEVEL: Passive

ANIMALS ... CONTINUED

RABBIT
Fluffy, but potentially deadly.

DROPS:

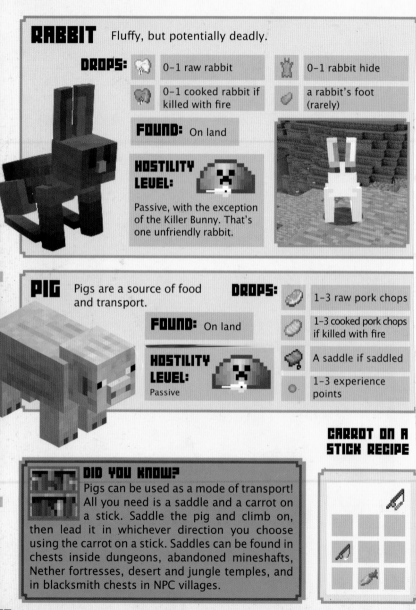

🍖	0-1 raw rabbit	🪆	0-1 rabbit hide
🍖	0-1 cooked rabbit if killed with fire	🦴	a rabbit's foot (rarely)

FOUND: On land

HOSTILITY LEVEL:

Passive, with the exception of the Killer Bunny. That's one unfriendly rabbit.

PIG
Pigs are a source of food and transport.

FOUND: On land

HOSTILITY LEVEL:
Passive

DROPS:

1-3 raw pork chops
1-3 cooked pork chops if killed with fire
A saddle if saddled
1-3 experience points

CARROT ON A STICK RECIPE

DID YOU KNOW?
Pigs can be used as a mode of transport! All you need is a saddle and a carrot on a stick. Saddle the pig and climb on, then lead it in whichever direction you choose using the carrot on a stick. Saddles can be found in chests inside dungeons, abandoned mineshafts, Nether fortresses, desert and jungle temples, and in blacksmith chests in NPC villages.

HORSE

Horses, donkeys, and mules can be tamed, and are one of the fastest methods of transport around.

FOUND:

Horses and donkeys are found in plains and savannas. Mules are created when a player breeds a horse with a donkey.

HOSTILITY LEVEL:

Passive

DROPS:

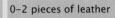	0–2 pieces of leather
	A saddle if saddled
	Horse armor if equipped
	Chest — plus contents — if equipped
	1–3 experience points

ANIMALS ...CONTINUED

WOLF
Wild wolves can be tamed, turning them into dogs. Make sure you don't hurt them, or they'll become hostile.

FOUND: In grassy areas in forests and taiga biomes

HOSTILITY LEVEL: Usually neutral

HOSTILITY LEVEL: Hostile when attacked

DROPS: 1–3 experience points

DID YOU KNOW? Wolves can be tamed with a few bones. (Skeletons drop bones when they die.) Once tamed, a red collar will appear on the wolf. It will attack whatever you're fighting, unless it's a creeper, in which case it will run for its life. Very sensible.

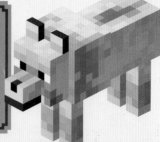

You can put tamed wolves on leads using fishing rods.

OCELOT

Wild ocelots can be tamed, turning them into cat companions.

DROPS: 1-3 experience points

FOUND: In jungles

HOSTILITY LEVEL: Passive

Ocelots transform into cute cats when tamed with fish. Both ocelots and cats will scare creepers away, so they make great companions.

BAT

Bats are the only passive mob able to fly.

FOUND: Anywhere in the Overworld

DROPS: Nothing

HOSTILITY LEVEL: Passive

Bats are unique. They're the only passive mob that spawn in the dark, and also the only passive mob that can fly.

SQUID

Despite their toothy appearance, squids are harmless and perfectly happy minding their own business.

HOSTILITY LEVEL: Passive

FOUND: In water

DROPS: 1-3 ink sacs

1-3 experience points

VILLAGERS

FARMER   **PRIEST**   **BUTCHER**   **BLACKSMITH**   **LIBRARIAN**

Villagers are human figures dressed in different clothing, depending on their jobs within the village.

FOUND: In NPC (Non-Player Character) villages, either wandering around or within different buildings, depending on their job. They spawn in the building that relates to their profession.

DROPS: Nothing, but they like to trade goods for emeralds

If you see a huge, iron creature lumbering around a village, don't be alarmed. It's just your friendly local iron golem, there to defend the villagers from hostile mob attacks. They spawn naturally in villages with 10 or more villagers and 21 or more doors. You can also craft them on the ground in front of you using 4 blocks of iron and a pumpkin head.

DID YOU KNOW? Villagers can breed, creating cute baby villagers. But sadly they only stay babies for 20 minutes, after which they become adults.

A GUIDE TO VILLAGER TRADING
BY CAPTAINSPARKLEZ

Select a villager and take a look at their trading menu. Adding items you are willing to trade on the left side of the arrow will result in an item appearing for the taking on the right. Emeralds will always be involved in a transaction, either as payment or as the item to be purchased. As a player continues to trade, the villagers will add more offers to their trade menus. You'll know a villager has added a new offer when a purple particle effect appears over their head. These offers can be accessed by selecting the buttons on the right or left of the trade menu. The cost of trades may seem quite high given the scarcity of emeralds, but villager trading is the only way to obtain items like chain-mail armor and bottle o' enchanting in Survival mode, so it's well worth doing.

TIP: Villages may also hold valuable loot. A quick search through the buildings may uncover items as rare as diamonds, and sometimes even the resources needed to complete a villager trade. There's nothing better than getting a villager to pay to recover his own items!

Villagers can be attacked by zombies and turned into zombie villagers. And baby villagers can be turned into terrifying baby zombie villagers. *Eek!*

CREEPER
(AKA CREEPUS EXPLODUS)

Creepers are one of the most dangerous mobs in the game. They will run toward you, then explode, possibly killing you and destroying everything in the surrounding area (e.g. the house that took you days to build). Creepers are almost completely silent, which makes it easy for them to take you by surprise. They hiss quietly just before they explode.

Creepers spawn in areas with a light level of 7 or less, but don't die when the sun rises. Instead they continue to creep around until killed. Lighting your house or shelter will stop creepers spawning inside.

WEAPONS:

HOSTILITY LEVEL:

Hostile

DID YOU KNOW? Notch accidentally invented the creeper when he was trying to make a pig.

HOW TO KILL:

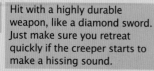

Shoot several times with a bow and arrows, from a distance

Try to make it fall from a height, e.g. off a cliff

Hit with a highly durable weapon, like a diamond sword. Just make sure you retreat quickly if the creeper starts to make a hissing sound.

Try to make it walk through lava

Blow up by luring into a hole filled with TNT

Try to make it walk into cacti

DROPS:

	Gunpowder, which you can use to make TNT
	Music discs if killed by a skeleton
	5 experience points

If a creeper is struck by lightning, it becomes a charged creeper, which will make it even more dangerous and explosive. Stay out of its way at all costs.

AN EARLY ENCOUNTER WITH A CREEPER
BY PAUL SOARES JR.

On my first world, I had a small home carved into the side of a hill. I built a balcony overlooking the front lawn. At night I would stand on the balcony and taunt the monsters below. I recall one particular night when a group of agitated creepers were beneath the balcony, but I was well out of their reach.

As I laughed and called them names, a creeper landed right next to me, having jumped down onto the balcony from a ledge above. I leaped away just as the creeper exploded and blew the balcony to pieces! I survived the blast but fell to the lawn below, smack-dab in the middle of the angry gang of creepers.

The moral of the story? Creepers always get the last laugh.

In Minecraft, the seemingly impossible is often possible, and that applies to hostile mobs as well as to you. Despite having no arms, creepers are still clever enough to climb ladders and vines. Don't say we didn't warn you!

LEVEL : 3 L T

Skeletons can move quickly and are armed with bows and arrows, which means they can kill you from a distance. They are fairly smart — they can climb ladders and will seek shelter from the sun where they can.

They spawn in areas with a light level of 7 or less, and you'll know a skeleton is nearby if you hear a rattly, almost musical sound.

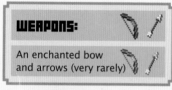

WEAPONS:

An enchanted bow and arrows (very rarely)

HOSTILITY LEVEL:

Hostile

HOW TO KILL:

	Shoot several times with a bow and arrows, from a distance
	Hit with a highly durable weapon, like a diamond sword, then retreat quickly
	Try to trap it in daylight. This will cause it to burst into flames.
	Try to make it fall from a height, e.g. off a cliff
	Try to make it walk through lava
	Try to make it walk into cacti

BOW AND ARROWS RECIPES

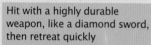

TIP: If you manage to kill a skeleton from 50 blocks away or more with a bow and arrows, you'll earn the Sniper Duel achievement as a reward.

DID YOU KNOW? Skeletons can shoot endermen with their arrows, which is something players can't do. However, this usually results in the enderman becoming hostile toward the skeleton and killing it shortly after.

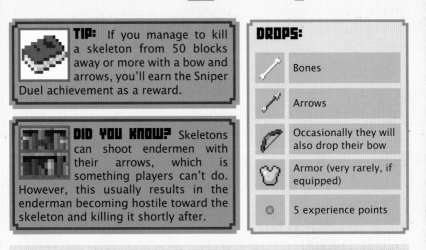

DROPS:

	Bones
	Arrows
	Occasionally they will also drop their bow
	Armor (very rarely, if equipped)
	5 experience points

HOW TO KILL A SKELETON
BY CAPTAINSPARKLEZ

The easiest way to kill a skeleton is to use its own weapon against it. Using a bow to fire arrows from a distance greatly reduces the chances of being hit in return. Because skeletons have the same health as a player, 3 shots from a fully charged bow will be enough to kill them.

If melee/hand-to-hand weapons are the only option, it is most efficient to use a sprint approach in a spiraling fashion, as the skeleton will have a greater chance of missing. Blocking with a sword before being struck by a skeleton's arrow will also reduce the damage it deals. Try to avoid picking a melee fight with a skeleton in the water, however, as the reduced player movement speed will make the skeleton even deadlier.

Skeletons have the ability to pick up and put on armor, mob heads, pumpkins, and jack-o'-lanterns. Any headgear a skeleton picks up will protect it from burning in sunlight, making it even more dangerous. Try not to let them get their bony hands on these items!

ZOMBIE

Zombies aren't much of a threat unless you bump into a large group of them, but they can repeatedly inflict damage just by touching you.

They spawn on solid blocks, in areas with a light level of 7 or less. You can usually hear them coming toward you since they make groaning noises when wandering and snarling noises when attacked or injured.

HOSTILITY LEVEL:
Hostile

TIP: Zombies will try to break down the door to your shelter. If it's a wooden door, they'll only succeed if your difficulty level is set to hard. But if it's an iron door their clumsy green fists will never manage to break through. Take that, zombies!

DID YOU KNOW? Some zombies can pick items up from the ground, and you can give a zombie items like swords, bones, and bows. Be warned: This will make the zombie highly dangerous.

HOW TO KILL:

	Shoot with a bow and arrows from a distance
	Hit repeatedly with a weapon until it dies
	Try to trap it in daylight, which will make it burst into flames. It will try to seek shade under a tree or in water, so this can be tricky.
	Try to make it fall from a height, e.g. off a cliff
	Try to make it walk through lava
	Try to make it walk into cacti

	If a zombie picks up any headgear, it will be protected from burning in the sun.

Some zombies spawn wearing armor and may drop some or all of it when killed.

DROPS:

	Rotten flesh. You can eat it, but there's a good chance you'll get food poisoning as a result!
	5 experience points
	Iron ingots (very rarely)
	Shovels (very rarely)
	Swords (very rarely)
	Carrots or potatoes (very rarely)

AN EARLY ENCOUNTER WITH A ZOMBIE
BY PAUL SOARES JR.

While recording a video tutorial about surviving underground, I had a near-death experience in a pool of lava. Quick thinking, fast reactions, and a bucket of water saved my life, so I was feeling good about having escaped death so expertly!

Later, when I spied a patch of redstone ore on a narrow ledge above the lava, I was confident that I could collect it despite the danger. Sure enough, I mined the redstone and was happily making my way back along the ledge when a zombie fell from above, landed at my side, and punched me! The blow knocked me off the ledge and into the lava pool, but this time my luck ran out and I was burned to a crisp.

The moral of the story? Don't get cocky!

SPIDER

Spiders are hostile when the light level around them is 9 or less, so they are only a threat to you at night or in dark areas. Once hostile, however, they will remain that way, even when day comes.

They spawn in areas with a light level of 9 or less and can see you through solid blocks. They can also climb walls and jump large distances. You can hear them coming as they make a hissing sound. Watch out for their red eyes glowing in the dark.

HOSTILITY LEVEL:
Neutral in daylight

HOSTILITY LEVEL:
Hostile in low light levels

HOW TO KILL:

	Shoot with a bow and arrows from a distance		Try to make it fall from a height, e.g. off a cliff
	Attack with a weapon like an axe or a sword		Try to make it walk through lava
	Set on fire with flint and steel		Try to make it walk into cacti

DROPS:

String, which can be used to make bows, fishing rods, and wool

5 experience points

Spider eyes when killed by a player directly, which can be used to make certain potions (very advanced stuff!)

HOW TO KILL A SPIDER
BY CAPTAINSPARKLEZ

The most efficient way to kill a spider is with well-timed blows from a sword, since it will continue to lunge toward a player once aggravated. With 16 units of health, a spider takes fewer hits to kill than a zombie, but its agility allows it to strike more often.

A bow and arrows can be effective from farther away, but in close combat, due to the bow's charge-up time, a spider will often land multiple attacks before you are able to fire off a kill shot.

DID YOU KNOW?
Occasionally a spider will spawn with a skeleton on its back, forming the dangerous spider jockey. This thing can jump, climb walls, and shoot at you with arrows. *Eek!*

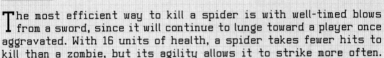

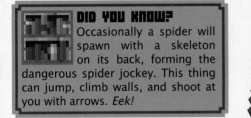

TIP: Unless you're wearing armor and have a bow and arrows, and plenty of space, you should make a run for it if you spot a spider jockey. It can kill you in seconds!

Endermen are rare neutral mobs, but they will attack you if provoked. You're in trouble if you attack them first or if you accidentally catch them in your crosshairs at night, since looking at an enderman from the upper legs upward is taken as a sign of hostility.

When an enderman attacks it will open its mouth and shake as it rushes toward you. They can teleport, too, which makes it almost impossible to escape from them. They can also pick up blocks and move them around.

They spawn in pairs, unlike other mobs, and can often be spotted at night in groups of up to five. They retreat underground during the day.

HOSTILITY LEVEL:
Neutral if left alone

HOSTILITY LEVEL:
Hostile if attacked

DID YOU KNOW? If you put on a pumpkin head, an enderman won't become hostile if you look at it. Weird but true!

TIP: An enderman's secret weapon is its ability to teleport around and take you by surprise. If you find yourself the object of an enderman's aggressive advances, it's best to get your back up against a solid surface like a wall or rock face as quickly as possible. This will make it impossible for the enderman to teleport directly behind you and catch you off guard with an attack.

HOW TO KILL:
It's no good shooting at an enderman with a bow and arrows. It will just teleport away before the arrow hits, so you need to be clever if you want to finish them off. Try one of these tactics instead:

	Lead it to water or throw water onto it using a bucket
	Try to make it fall from a height of 44 blocks or more
	Try to make it walk through lava
	Try to make it walk into cacti

DROPS:

	Ender pearls. You can use an ender pearl to craft an eye of ender.
	5 experience points

Because of their ability to pick up blocks, endermen can create iron golems or snow golems if they pick up a pumpkin and place it on top of 2 stacked blocks of iron or snow respectively.

AN EARLY ENCOUNTER WITH AN ENDERMAN
BY PAUL SOARES JR.

Ah, the enderman. A perfect gentleman . . . until you look him in the eye! I remember when endermen didn't exist, which made my first encounter with one all the more terrifying. At that time, I had countless victories against the many familiar monsters under my belt. I felt like the unrivaled champion of the realm. And then I met an enderman. It was dusk, and I was strolling through a field, with no small swagger, when I suddenly spotted a strange figure in the distance. It was tall and thin and black as night, with unnaturally long limbs. I was creeped out for sure, but it paid me no heed so I crept closer to get a better look.

The creature wandered about aimlessly, carrying a block of dirt in its long arms. It did not appear to be hostile. I continued to observe the creepy fellow for another few moments and that's when it happened. It turned to face me and I looked right into its eyes! It let out a terrible screech and began to tremble, but remained fixed where it stood, glaring at me. I freaked out and ran away from it. Then I heard a *zzzpp* sound and suddenly the thing was on me, attacking, again and again! It was too fast and I had no time to react. Then the world around me faded out . . . I was dead.

The moral of the story? Looks can be deceiving . . . and deadly.

Endermites sometimes spawn when an enderman teleports from one location to another, or when a player throws an ender pearl. They are small, hostile, buglike creatures that look like silverfish. They have a single red eye, and emit a purple particle effect, much like the endermen themselves. They despawn within 2 minutes.

Endermen have a 15% chance of spawning an endermite when they teleport, but this drops off by 1% each time they spawn one.

When endermites appear, endermen will immediately attack them. Endermites will attack players within 16 blocks and will do 2 damage per hit.

HOSTILITY LEVEL:

Hostile

DROPS ⦿ 3 experience points

HOW TO KILL

Build a 2-block-tall tower and attack them from above so they can't damage you

Lead them to soul sand. They'll sink into it and suffocate.

DID YOU KNOW? If for some reason you decide to name an endermite using a name tag, it'll live until it is killed. Name tags can't be crafted but can be found in naturally generated chests, and can sometimes be caught when fishing. To attach, select it in your hotbar and use it on your chosen endermite, then type in a name.

SILVERFISH

Silverfish spawn from monster spawners in strongholds, as well as from special stonelike blocks called monster eggs found in strongholds and underground in extreme hills biomes. These small, buglike creatures can really cause you some grief.

They will appear if you try to mine a monster egg block. When unearthed, a silverfish will immediately attack you, dealing half a heart of damage per hit. And if you attack them, any silverfish in the surrounding area will wake and join in. They really are best avoided if possible.

The problem is, monster egg blocks take slightly longer to mine than regular stone blocks, but are otherwise identical so you can easily mine them by accident.

HOW TO KILL

Build a 2-block-tall tower and attack them from above so they can't damage you

Lead them to soul sand. They'll sink into it and suffocate.

Try hitting them with a diamond sword — if killed in a single hit, nearby silverfish won't be alerted.

HOSTILITY LEVEL:

Hostile

DROPS

5 experience points

TIP: To reduce the chance of being overcome by silverfish when mining, make your mines as wide and open as possible. That way you won't back yourself into a corner.

LEVEL: SLIME

Slimes can be large, medium, or tiny in size, and their health points decrease as they get smaller. They can see you through solid blocks, and will hop toward you and bump into you repeatedly until you die.

Large and medium slimes can deal a fair amount of damage. Tiny slimes can only damage you by pushing you off a cliff or into lava. You can hear them coming by the slapping sound they make. When killed, they will separate into smaller slimes (except for tiny slimes, which will drop slimeballs instead).

Slimes spawn deep underground (below level 40) in any light level and on the surface of swamps in areas with a light level of 8 or less.

HOSTILITY LEVEL:
Hostile

HOW TO KILL:

🏹	Shoot with a bow and arrows from a distance	◈	Try to make it fall from a height, e.g. off a cliff
🗡	Attack with a weapon like an axe or a sword	▦	Try to make it hop into lava
🌵	Try to make it hop into cacti		

DID YOU KNOW? Once they've spotted you, slimes will head straight for you regardless of the direction you're traveling. This means you can lead them into danger to get rid of them. Try leading them into lava or over a cliff.

66

Tiny slimes will drop 0-2 slimeballs, which can be used to make magma cream (used in brewing potions) and sticky pistons (used to move blocks)

Tiny slimes will drop 1 experience point, medium slimes will drop 2 experience points, and large slimes will drop 4 experience points

HOW TO KILL A SLIME
BY CAPTAINSPARKLEZ

So long as a player keeps a reasonable distance from the slimes, they remain relatively easy to kill. When attacking a slime of the largest size, always bear in mind that it will split once enough damage has been dealt, and keep a safe distance to avoid being swarmed. Because only the larger slimes can deal damage to a player, it's best to focus attacks on those before moving on to the smallest ones.

PROFILE: WITCH

Witches are highly dangerous. They use splash potions against players and, cunningly, drink helpful potions to protect themselves. This makes them the only non-boss mob that can heal.

When damaged, they drink a potion of healing; when set on fire, a potion of fire resistance; when submerged in water, a potion of water breathing; and when far away from you, a potion of swiftness.

Just when you thought it couldn't get any worse, witches aren't vulnerable to sunlight, either.

They spawn in the Overworld when the light level is 7 or less, often in witch huts in swamplands.

DID YOU KNOW? Witches are the only silent hostile mob. Yep — you can't even hear them coming.

TIP: Witches can't attack while they're healing themselves, so take advantage when they're drinking defensive potions and get some hits in.

HOSTILITY LEVEL:
Hostile

WEAPONS:

DROPS

	Glass bottles
	Glowstone dust
	Gunpowder
	Redstone dust
	Spider eyes
	Sticks
	Sugar
	5 experience points

HOW TO KILL

Use a bow and arrows to take the witch out while standing out of range of its splash potions

Hit it with a sword

It's a good idea to keep a bucket of milk in your hotbar when fighting a witch. If you drink it, any potion status effects will be nullified.

Found in ocean monuments, as their name suggests, guardians exist to guard.

They spawn inside the ocean monuments and can be found in all chambers as well as outside. They're equipped with lasers to deal damage to any intruders as well as to squid in the surrounding area.

HOSTILITY LEVEL:

Hostile

WEAPONS: Laser and body spikes

HOW TO KILL:

Try to corner it and hit it repeatedly with a diamond sword

Use a fishing rod to pull it out of the water and onto land, where you can hit it with a diamond sword much more easily

DROPS:

	0–1 raw fish
	0–1 prismarine crystals
	0–2 prismarine shards
	Clownfish
	Pufferfish
	Raw salmon

DID YOU KNOW?

You won't be able to dodge a guardian's laser beam, but if you're quick, you might be able to block it with another solid block.

PROFILE: ELDER GUARDIAN

Elder guardians are stronger versions of guardians and found in the center of monuments.

Unlike regular guardians, elder guardians can inflict mining fatigue III on players. They tend to be found around the central chamber, guarding the most valuable treasure — the gold blocks.

HOSTILITY LEVEL:

Hostile

WEAPONS: Laser and body spikes

HOW TO KILL:

🗡️	Try to corner it and hit it repeatedly with a diamond sword
🎣	Use a fishing rod to pull it out of the water and onto land, where you can hit it with a diamond sword much more easily

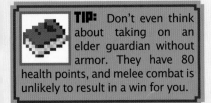

TIP: Don't even think about taking on an elder guardian without armor. They have 80 health points, and melee combat is unlikely to result in a win for you.

DROPS:

🐟	0-1 raw fish
	0-1 prismarine crystals
	0-2 prismarine shards
	Clownfish
	Pufferfish
	Raw salmon
	Wet sponge when killed by a player

CAPTAINSPARKLEZ
MY FIRST DAY IN MINECRAFT
SURVIVAL SINGLE PLAYER (SSP)

My first experience with Minecraft came in the summer of 2010, when the game was still in its Alpha phase. I had been encouraged by a friend to try it, and began my experience with the browser-based multiplayer Creative mode. For a few days I experimented with the browser-based version before realizing there was a downloadable client for single-player Survival mode. I had only watched a couple of Minecraft videos on YouTube at this point, and possessed only the most basic knowledge regarding overall gameplay strategy, but I decided to take the plunge.

I loaded up the game and generated a new world. My character ended up on a hillside next to a beach, with a very sparse supply of trees. I had a limited understanding of the tasks a player should strive to accomplish before day's end and a distinct lack of understanding of time allocation, so I decided to begin by exploring. Needless to say, my priorities were slightly out of order. Rather than beginning by harvesting the small amount of wood around my spawn point, I set off to find the coolest natural formation I could to claim it as my home base.

After about ten minutes of exploration, I stumbled upon an overhang formation that I was happy to call home. The only problem was that with less than 5 minutes of daylight remaining and no trees in sight, I was in a bit of a bind. Panic set in. I had found this great location to set up shop, but now I'd be forced to abandon it in search of wood.

I found a few trees relatively quickly, but night was approaching fast. Due to my lack of experience, I ended up with only a set of wooden tools before nightfall, and nothing more. As soon as night hit I realized my biggest mistake. I had forgotten to collect coal. No coal meant no torches, which meant I was completely blind in the dark.

Up until the Adventure Update, night was pitch-black. No brightness slider, no natural moonlight. I stood helpless in the pitch-dark, listening to the faint sound of zombies in the distance. Thinking they were coming to attack me, I began to walk for my life. Not realizing that so long as you stand still, mobs won't spawn  within 24 blocks of you and they won't pursue you until they are even closer, in retrospect I realize this only further aggravated the situation.

Things spiraled downhill pretty quickly from there. An arrow from a skeleton I couldn't see, punches from a zombie vaguely outlined in front of my face, attacks from a spider, all leading up to the dreaded hiss-boom from a creeper that sent me to the respawn screen.

With no beds in Alpha, I was sent back to my coastal hillside spawn to search again for my short-lived home base. This time, however, I'd be sure to do things differently, so as not to let history repeat itself!

youtube.com/captainsparklez

IMPROVE YOUR SHELTER
IN FIVE EASY STEPS

Now that you've made it through your first few nights, it's time to make some home improvements. You need to make your shelter as strong and secure as possible, while ensuring you can see what's going on outside.

Try these 5 easy steps to turn your emergency shelter into a home you can be proud of.

1 EXPAND

Dig farther into your rock face to create more room and/or build outward at the front of your shelter.

2 CRAFT WOODEN DOORS

These will keep you safe from hostile mobs (except for zombies if your difficulty is set to hard).

3 CRAFT WINDOWS

Smelt sand in your furnace to make glass, then replace parts of your walls with glass blocks to create basic windows.

LADDER RECIPE

Three ladders can be crafted from 7 sticks. Ladders can be placed on the side of blocks.

5 START A MINE

Create the entrance to your mine inside your shelter so you will always be able to exit into your own home. Just remember to light it up or hostile mobs will join you as you hunt for valuable ores!

4 ADD MORE TORCHES

This will prevent hostile mobs from spawning and will make your home easier to find at night. Placing torches outside your home means you can see hostiles coming, too.

Ah, gardening. Such a relaxing and enjoyable pastime. Now that you've made yourself a real home, why not create a little garden to enjoy on sunny days?

1 FENCE RECIPE

First, fence off an area to use as your garden. Right next to your home is ideal. That way it's on your doorstep and you can shoot inside your shelter if you spot a hostile mob.

Now lay out a path using either wood planks or stone. Then collect flowers and tree saplings, and plant them in your garden.

Create a pond by digging a hole, then collecting water from a nearby water source with a bucket. If you can find them, add some lily pads.

4 | BENCH RECIPE

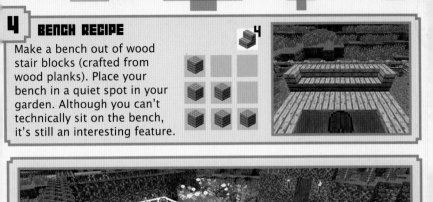

Make a bench out of wood stair blocks (crafted from wood planks). Place your bench in a quiet spot in your garden. Although you can't technically sit on the bench, it's still an interesting feature.

With a little bit of time and practice, you could have a garden like this!

MY FIRST GARDEN
BY PAUL SOARES JR.

Back in the old days of Minecraft Alpha, we didn't have all of the fancy landscaping options that you have now. Gardeners today have access to flowerpots, hedges, colorful slabs, stone walls, mossy steps, lily pads, ferns, vines, tall grass, and more!

Alas, my first garden was a plain and sad-looking affair with a gravel path bordered by red and yellow flowers, and surrounded by a wooden fence. Despite its blandness I was rather proud of my little garden, though I don't think my neighbors shared my enthusiasm. In fact, they seemed almost offended and were bent on its destruction, but what do you expect when your neighbors are creepers? In the end, my neighbors got what they desired and my garden was transformed into a gaping crater. Probably for the best . . .

And the moral of the story? Sometimes blessings are disguised as creeper craters.

FARMING CROPS

Having your own farm ensures you always have a reliable food source near your shelter. You can grow crops like wheat, melons, pumpkins, carrots, and potatoes by turning dirt into farmland.

WHEAT FARM TUTORIAL

1

First, you're going to need some wheat seeds. Find some tall grass and destroy it. It will drop between 0–1 wheat seeds.

DID YOU KNOW?

You can also collect 0–3 wheat seeds by destroying full-grown wheat, which can often be found growing in NPC village farms.

2

HOE RECIPE

Next, you'll need to till some dirt blocks to make them into farmland. To till dirt you will need a wooden hoe.

3

Use your pickaxe to hack out several strips of blocks, each separated by a row of dirt blocks. Fill the strips with water using a bucket. Then use your hoe to till the rows of dirt blocks.

4

Plant wheat seeds in the tilled earth. Fence off your farm to protect it.

5

Wheat goes through 8 stages of growth. You can harvest wheat at any time by using any tool on it, but this will only yield wheat crop when it is in the final stage of growth. Wheat can be used to breed animals (see the next page), and can be crafted into bread, cake, and cookies (see page 37). *Yum!*

If you plant your wheat seeds on hydrated blocks of farmland, they will grow quickly, but if you can't find water, wheat seeds will eventually grow on unhydrated blocks, too.

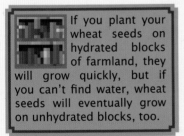

BONE MEAL RECIPE

3

Adding bone meal to your crops will bring them to their full-grown state immediately. You can make bone meal by putting bones on a crafting grid.

TIP: Light helps wheat grow, so put torches next to your wheat farm to help it along at night.

Growing melons, pumpkins, carrots, and potatoes is very similar to growing wheat. Just plant them in your farmland and wait for them to grow.

BREEDING ANIMALS

You can use food to encourage passive animals of the same species to breed, producing cute baby animals! Animals won't respawn when killed, so breeding also ensures the survival of the species.

Once fed, an animal will enter love mode. If a nearby animal of the same species is also in love mode, the pair will breed. You'll know an animal is in love mode when little red hearts appear out of the top of its head.

The two animals will look like they're kissing for a moment and red hearts will continue to appear. When they break apart an adorable baby animal will be standing between them! *Aww . . .*

The item of food needed to encourage animals to breed varies depending on the species. Most animals respond to just one type of food.

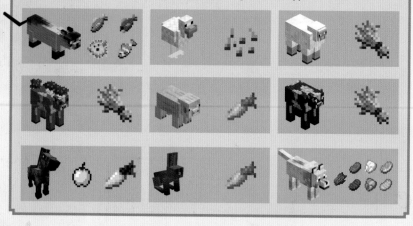

Blue and pink don't mix, but red and yellow do!

A baby animal will follow its parents around for 20 minutes before getting bored and wandering off to do its own thing.

TIP: Animals in love mode will need to be fairly near to each other to breed, and often don't notice each other if they aren't close enough. If you're in a large open area, build a pen and herd them inside first.

Once an animal has bred, it won't be able to enter love mode again for 5 minutes.

ARMOR

As you know by now, the world of Minecraft is a tough place. Fortunately, you can craft a helmet, a chest plate, trousers, and boots to protect yourself and increase your defense points.

Wearing armor will provide you with a level of protection from certain common forms of damage, as follows:

- mob attack
- enemy player attack
- touching fire or lava
- touching cacti
- explosions
- lightning
- falling anvils

Cool people don't look at explosions.

TIP: You can get all types of armor, except for gold armor, through villager trading.

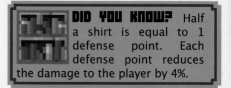

DID YOU KNOW? Half a shirt is equal to 1 defense point. Each defense point reduces the damage to the player by 4%.

TYPES OF ARMOR

Armor can be crafted from leather, iron, gold, or diamond. Each substance offers a different level of protection, with leather armor being the weakest and diamond the strongest.

CRAFTING ARMOR

You will need 24 units of your chosen material to make a full set of armor. Let's use iron armor as an example.

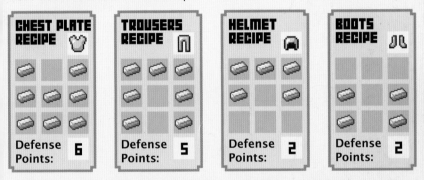

CHEST PLATE RECIPE
Defense Points: **6**

TROUSERS RECIPE
Defense Points: **5**

HELMET RECIPE
Defense Points: **2**

BOOTS RECIPE
Defense Points: **2**

You'll see 4 armor slots in the top left corner of your inventory. Drag your crafted armor into the appropriate slot, and it will appear on your body. Remember: As armor absorbs damage, its durability decreases. Eventually, it will have no durability left, and you'll need to craft a new set.

Your armor bar will automatically appear above your health bar as soon as you're wearing armor. Keep an eye on it to check how much durability is left in your current armor and make sure you have a replacement set ready for when it gets low.

Chain-mail armor also exists, although this can't be crafted.

You can only get chain-mail armor if a mob is wearing it and then drops it, or through trading with villagers.

EXPLORING

Now that you're becoming familiar with the game, it's time to test your survival skills and explore a little farther from the comfort of home.

Try these exploration tips to get you started and minimize your chances of getting lost.

BEACON

Mark your shelter with a beacon. Paul Soares Jr. created a simple beacon from a tower of dirt blocks and a torch, and this design is now widely used in Minecraft.

TORCHES

Leave a trail of torches to light your path back home. This will be particularly useful for finding your way at night.

1 To build your beacon, create a tower of blocks by using the pillar jumping technique: jump, then quickly place a dirt block directly below your feet. Then do the same in the block next to you, and repeat until you are standing on top of a tall pillar, 2 dirt blocks wide.

2 Place a torch on top of one tower, then dig down in the other tower to get back to ground level safely. A beacon can be particularly handy at night to guide you home.

TIP: Before you explore, place any valuable items you don't need in your chest, so you won't lose them if you die.

ROAD BUILDING

Make a road out of cobblestone so you can follow it home. This is a fun option if you like constructing and building.

SIGN RECIPE

Place signs on the ground. A screen will pop up asking you to enter some text. You can add text to tell you where you are, and arrows to lead you back to your shelter.

Finding Your Way

There are several handheld pieces of equipment that will help keep you on track. A compass, a map, and a clock will come in handy if you find yourself in unfamiliar territory.

The sun and moon rise in the east and set in the west, so you can always use them to figure out which direction you are traveling in.

COMPASS RECIPE

Compasses point to your spawn point. You can craft a compass from iron ingots and redstone dust.

CLOCK RECIPE

Craft a clock from gold ingots and redstone dust to tell you whether it's day or night when you're underground.

WHAT TO TAKE WITH YOU:

	Lots of food items
	Lots of weapons
	As many torches as possible
	A bed. If you can manage to hop in and fall asleep before being attacked, you'll skip the night and wake up at the beginning of the next day.

TIP: Use the sneak function when exploring along the top of cliffs to ensure you don't fall off the edge. See pages 14–17 to find out how to do this.

MAP RECIPE

Make a map from paper and a compass so you can get a sense of direction and see where you are in relation to your shelter.

MINECART SYSTEM

The world of Minecraft seems to be never-ending! Crafting a basic minecart system will make it easier to travel long distances, transport items, and help you to explore your surroundings.

RAIL RECIPE

16

Rails are crafted using sticks and iron ingots.

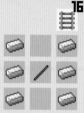

Once you have enough rails, place them on the ground to create a track. If you change direction when laying track, the previous piece of rail will automatically form a corner. If you place track over a step in the landscape, the track will automatically connect.

MINECART RECIPE

Smelt 5 blocks of iron ore in a furnace to give you 5 iron ingots, which will make a minecart.

Place a basic minecart on your track and push it to get going, then jump on board when it reaches a decent speed. When using a basic minecart it's a good idea to start your track on a hill. The momentum of traveling down the hill will give your cart extra power.

MINECART WITH CHEST RECIPE

You can make a storage minecart from a minecart and a chest.

MINECART WITH FURNACE RECIPE

You can make a powered minecart from a minecart and a furnace.

Now craft either another basic minecart (to sit in) or a storage minecart (to place items in). Place this on the track in front of the powered minecart, then add coal or charcoal to the powered minecart to get it going.

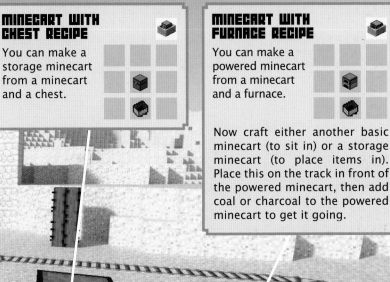

EXCLUSIVE INTERVIEW

WITH NOTCH AND JEB

Despite the fact they are both very busy and important, we managed to pin down Notch and Jeb for an exclusive interview about Minecraft.

Here's what they had to say about working on one of the most popular games ever created.

HOW DID YOU LEARN THE SKILLS TO MAKE MINECRAFT?

Programming was one of my interests as a child. I kept working at it because it was fun. I had a Commodore 128 — an ancient computer! I was programming in BASIC. I made games as a hobby, went to school, and made some friends. We helped one another learn and develop, but I always kept it as a hobby. Minecraft actually started as a hobby project.

I started out changing examples in QBasic on a PC with Windows 3.1. I think I learned most things by spending a lot of time programming. I was 11 or 12 when I started, but I didn't do anything useful until I was 17 or 18. That's when I understood what I was doing and could create my own games instead of changing other examples. The Internet hadn't really taken off when I was growing up, so I bought some books and tried to learn from them by copying from the book and typing it in.

NOTCH, WHAT'S YOUR FAVORITE FEATURE IN MINECRAFT?

I think the infinite terrain is fun, but redstone is a lot of fun, too. It gives you the chance to program your own things within the game. The first computer blew me away. People have made some really cool games within Minecraft. Someone made Duck Hunt. Someone made an entire Team Fortress 2 mod in vanilla Minecraft with redstone!

JEB, YOU'VE ADDED A LOT OF THINGS TO MINECRAFT — WHICH ONE IS YOUR FAVORITE?

The random structures, like strongholds and Nether fortresses. It was challenging to do — when they're generated, the game doesn't know what the terrain looks like. The game has to make a lot of assumptions, which may result in villages with ravines running through them, or villages that are half-submerged in water.

NOTCH, WHAT PART OF MINECRAFT ARE YOU MOST PROUD OF?

The infinite terrain was very difficult to make. It's generated pseudo-randomly, which means that it's kind of random but always the same if you use the same starting seed. It has to generate the same terrain no matter which side you approach it from, and link into itself seamlessly. It was very complicated to get it working and a big change to make so far into development.

I think Jeb has a real talent for making procedurally generated structures like villages, Nether fortresses, and mines. He really makes those feel adventurous. I really like the way he's done that over the course of development.

JEB, WHICH PART OF MINECRAFT ARE YOU MOST PROUD OF?

I think one of the most amazing things about Minecraft is how it has brought people together to work toward a bigger goal, and lets them have fun together. That's the part of the game Notch created.

INTERVIEW ... CONTINUED

DID YOU EVER THINK MINECRAFT WOULD BECOME AS BIG AS IT IS NOW?

No! I thought it was pretty fun, so the original plan was to work on the game for half a year, sell it, make enough money to work on one or two more games, and keep doing that. I thought that Minecraft might make enough money for one or two games, but nothing like this, where we have an entire company behind it. It's grown a lot bigger than I thought it would.

Not really. When I started working on Minecraft it had sold 700,000 copies. We were still in Alpha stage, and we were about to go to Beta stage. We all thought that once we reached Beta and put the game up to full price, the sales would drop, then we would finish the game and start something else. The sales did drop for about a week or so, but that was just people buying lots of Alpha copies before we changed the price. Now it's at a stable 10,000 copies per day.

AND WHY DO YOU THINK MINECRAFT HAS BEEN SUCH A MASSIVE SUCCESS?

I don't know! I think maybe the simple graphics make it more universal. In photorealistic games you have to pick an audience, because that's what suits them best. But if you have simple graphics and simple game mechanics, you can make it complex if you want, but the basics of picking up and placing blocks make it more universal than other games.

At first you run around and try a few things. Then you think, *Ooh — I'm gonna build the biggest building that has ever been created!* Then you spend a long time doing that. Then you realize everybody else has been doing the same thing!

It gives people the ability to create something from their imaginations. But also, while you're creating it, it feels like you're actually in that world. It feels real somehow. Being able to share and cooperate with others also improves the experience.

A tower bridge from the master builders known as FyreUK.

WHAT DOES MINECRAFT MEAN TO YOU? IS IT MORE THAN A GAME?

Yeah! The community around Minecraft is what I think of as Minecraft these days. It's more than just a game. If you look on YouTube, Twitch.tv, blogs, and forums, there's so much content being produced by the community, and people are talking about and looking at what other people are doing. I think it's probably one of the most amazing gaming communities I've ever seen.

Yes. When I see young people playing Minecraft I realize it's also a learning tool. Plus it's had some cultural impact: the creeper face, books, and documentaries. And, of course, Block by Block, the UN–Habitat project. (Check out blockbyblock.org for more information.)

ACHIEVEMENT-

inecraft takes note of your achievements as you play. Keep an eye out for this pop-up box; it will appear briefly in the corner of your screen when you pass an important milestone.

Achievement get!
Cow tipper

Here are ten key achievements to aim for in your first few days:

 ### GETTING WOOD
Hit a tree until you get a block of wood.

 ### BENCHMARKING
Make a crafting table from 4 planks of wood.

 ### TIME TO MINE!
Use 2 sticks and 3 planks to make a wooden pickaxe.

HOT TOPIC
Use 8 blocks of stone to craft a furnace.

 ### ACQUIRE HARDWARE
Smelt a block of iron ore in your furnace to get an iron ingot.

 ### TIME TO FARM!
Craft a wooden hoe from 2 sticks and 2 wooden planks.

 ### GETTING AN UPGRADE
Improve on your wooden pickaxe by making one with a stone head.

 ### TIME TO STRIKE!
Use a stick and 2 planks to make a wooden sword.

 ### MONSTER HUNTER
Do battle with and defeat a hostile mob.

 ### COW TIPPER
Harvest some leather from a cow. Poor cow!

USEFUL LINKS

Congratulations! You've made it to the end of the Minecraft Essential Handbook, which means you're no longer a beginner but an advanced player. Now the fun can really begin!

Check out this list of useful websites. They'll really help you take your Minecrafting to the next level.

Official Minecraft website:
https://minecraft.net

Official Mojang website:
https://mojang.com

Minecraft wiki:
www.minecraftwiki.net

Official Facebook page:
www.facebook.com/minecraft

Mojang Team's YouTube channel:
www.youtube.com/teammojang

Official Minecraft Twitter page:
https://twitter.com/mojang

Notch's official Twitter page:
https://twitter.com/notch

Jeb's official Twitter page:
https://twitter.com/jeb_

Some other Minecraft sites, not monitored by Mojang or Scholastic. Enter at your own risk!

Creative community fansite Planet Minecraft:
www.planetminecraft.com

The Skindex -- for all your Minecraft fashion needs:
www.minecraftskins.com

Texture packs:
www.minecrafttexturepacks.com

Minecraft on Reddit:
www.reddit.com/r/Minecraft/

Paul Soares Jr.'s YouTube channel:
www.youtube.com/paulsoaresjr

CaptainSparklez' YouTube channel:
www.youtube.com/captainsparklez

(See page 7 for our Stay Safe Online policy.)

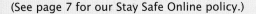

7/18 marking inside front cover. AS